The
WAY
of the
WISE

For foreign and subsidiary rights, contact the author.

Cover design by: Sara Young
Cover photo by: David Carvajal

ISBN: 978-1-964794-58-7   1 2 3 4 5 6 7 8 9 10

Printed in the United States of America

VOLUME 1

The WAY *of the* WISE

A DAILY WALK THROUGH THE BOOK OF PROVERBS

ARROWS & STONES

CONTENTS

A TRADITION OF TRUTH

Many years ago, when I was just a child, my grandmother encouraged me to read one proverb a day since the chapters correspond with the days of the month. She told me, "Brandon, it's easy! You'll always know what to read if you know the date!" Throughout my life, I have applied this practice to my time in the Word, and the proverbs have taught me so much along the way. I pray that my time in His Word bears fruit that will encourage you in your own time with Him! From God to Solomon, and from my grandmother, Maxine, to me, I now pass the tradition on to you! God Bless!

Day 1

BE CAREFUL WHAT
YOU WORK FOR

Have you ever heard the saying, "You don't always get what you want?" Well, according to Proverbs, that's debatable. Maybe we do get what we want—we just haven't been honest about what *it* is!

Proverb of the Day

> *Since they hated knowledge and did not choose to fear the LORD. Since they would not accept my advice and spurned my rebuke, they will eat the fruit of their ways and be filled with the fruit of their schemes.*
> —*Proverbs 1:29-31 (NIVUK)*

As this Proverb expresses, we tend to get what we want because what we want gets our effort. So, the real question is: what's getting our effort?

> *Satisfaction isn't based on tangible items but on a spiritual mindset.*

If it's the ways of God, then the ways of God lead to a life that produces the fruit of the Spirit: love, joy, peace, patience, kindness, goodness, faithfulness, gentleness, and self-control. Are you producing this fruit? We all claim to want it, but are we willing to put in the effort to produce it? Let's choose to put in the effort that produces the fruit we say we want—a fruit worthy of the Lord!

JOURNAL

_____

_____

_____

_____

_____

_____

_____

_____

_____

_____

_____

_____

_____

Day 2

DON'T TURN DOWN THE OFFER

Has anyone ever offered you a handshake, but you didn't return the gesture? That person made you an offer, but you chose not to make the same effort because you didn't feel inclined to reciprocate. The deal was not sealed.

Proverb of the Day

> *My son, if you accept My words and store up My commands within you . . . then you will understand the fear of the LORD and find the knowledge of God.*
> *—Proverbs 2:1, 5 (NIVUK)*

Wouldn't it be incredible to have access to God's knowledge and understanding of His wonder?

> *We just need to accept the offer and seal the deal!*

Well, God is extending His hand to make you that offer and seal the deal; all you need to do is reach back and take hold. This is what He has done through His Word, His Son, and through the Holy Spirit. God has extended all of who He is to us; we just need to accept the offer and seal the deal! Don't miss out on the most significant opportunity that will ever be offered to you!

JOURNAL

Day 3

THE POWER OF APPRECIATION

Have you ever had the opportunity to bless someone when they gave their best? Every day, we encounter people who barely make an effort, but we can't allow their lack of effort to rob those who do.

Proverb of the Day

Do not withhold good from those who deserve it when it's in your power to help them.

—Proverbs 3:27 (NLT)

We should strive to show appreciation to those who give their best and operate with selflessness. Often, good deeds go unnoticed, so we should acknowledge them when we see them!

> *Let's strive to help others keep going.*

We all know how it feels to be appreciated, but we also know how it feels when we're not. When appreciation is withheld, we struggle to continue our efforts, but when appreciation is shown, we're motivated to keep going. So, let's strive to help others keep going, and in turn, maybe someone else will encourage us to keep going, too!

JOURNAL

_____

_____

_____

_____

_____

_____

_____

_____

_____

_____

_____

_____

_____

_____

Day 4

TAKE WISDOM WITH YOU

Have you ever owned something that went with you everywhere you went? It was the one thing you never left behind because of the value it brought to your life.

Proverb of the Day

Do not forsake wisdom, and she will protect you; love her, and she will watch over you.

—*Proverbs 4:6 (NIVUK)*

Every day, we head out into the world, bringing along the things essential to our lives: our wallets, car keys, purses, watches, and many other things. When we leave those things behind, we often feel lost, sometimes even vulnerable.

> *Take some time and ensure that you have His Word with you.*

You've probably heard the saying, "I feel naked without it." This is how we should feel about God's wisdom: lost and vulnerable. However, until we include it in our daily lives, it will never become an essential part of it. Just keep in mind that it's the one item we can carry with us that will add more value than any other item we own. So, take some time and ensure that you have His Word with you before you go!

JOURNAL

_____

_____

_____

_____

_____

_____

_____

_____

_____

_____

_____

_____

Day 5

THE COST OF COMPARISON

Have you ever gotten caught up in the comparison game? You see what someone else has, and jealousy sets in. Comparison can easily blind us to our own blessings, making it seem as though the grass is greener on the other side.

Proverb of the Day

> *Drink water from your own cistern, and running water from your own well.*
> —*Proverbs 5:15 (BSB)*

In the surrounding verses, God encourages us to remain pure in our relationship with our spouse and to not allow another person's life to distract and lead us to our great downfall. But we can also experience similar downfalls when we take our eyes off our own blessings.

> *The grass is greenest where you water it!*

No matter the item, the opportunity, the person, or the subject, comparison robs us of what we already have, ultimately leaving us with nothing. So, choose to be grateful for what you have been given, and you'll see your increase come through your appreciation and honor. Remember, the grass is greenest where you water it!

JOURNAL

_____

_____

_____

_____

_____

_____

_____

_____

_____

_____

_____

_____

Day 6

DON'T GO BURNING YOURSELF

Have you ever been burned before? Probably so, but have you ever been burned on purpose? The answer to that is less likely to be a yes. Why would you burn yourself on purpose? It makes no sense!

Proverb of the Day

Can a man walk on hot coals without his feet being scorched?

—Proverbs 6:28 (NIVUK)

We read that question and immediately know the answer. But this question isn't meant to be answered—it's meant to provoke thought.

> *Choose today to know His path so that you don't get burned!*

Anyone who reads it would naturally say no, yet each day, many of us purposely walk down paths that will burn us. This doesn't have to happen! If we would apply God's Word to our lives, we would stay away from the path of sin—just as we would avoid a path of hot coals! So, choose today to know His path so that you don't get burned!

JOURNAL

_____

_____

_____

_____

_____

_____

_____

_____

_____

_____

_____

_____

_____

Day 7

THE ULTIMATE CON ARTIST

Have you ever been conned before? If so, you don't usually realize it until it's too late and costs you something. You wonder, "How did I fall for this? I thought I was smarter than that!" The realization of what's happened causes your stomach to turn.

Proverb of the Day

The woman approached him, seductively dressed and sly of heart.

—Proverbs 7:10 (NLT)

When it comes to conning, none is better than Satan.

> *Learn what you need to learn before it's too late and costs you more than you can afford!*

He carries the title of a thief for a reason, and we need to know that a thief doesn't always operate in the shadows but often out in plain sight where we're most vulnerable and trusting. This is why God's Word shows us the benefit of being aware of the devil's schemes. So, you must take the time to learn what you need to learn before it's too late and costs you more than you can afford!

JOURNAL

_____

_____

_____

_____

_____

_____

_____

_____

_____

_____

_____

_____

_____

_____

Day 8

WHEN HE CALLS YOUR NAME

Have you ever heard a parent call your name? It's always incredible how we respond to familiar voices in any place and at any time.

Proverb of the Day

I call to you, to all of you! I raise my voice to all people.
—*Proverbs 8:4 (NLT)*

When a parent calls our name, our response is less about what we've heard and more about knowing the voice of the call.

> *We respond because the voice we hear is familiar.*

Anyone can say our name and draw our attention, but it's the voice that causes us to respond. We respond because the voice we hear is familiar. Jesus says that His sheep—His followers—know His voice, so being familiar with His voice is an important part of recognizing whether we belong to Him or not! God says He calls out to all of us, so the question is: *Are you familiar enough* with His voice that you'll respond when He does?

JOURNAL

_____

_____

_____

_____

_____

_____

_____

_____

_____

_____

_____

_____

_____

_____

Day 9

LOUD AND UNAWARE

Have you ever known someone who talks really loud? Everything they say is on max volume, but what's crazy is that they rarely realize it. Now, have you ever been told you're being too loud? Chances are, you didn't realize it either.

Proverb of the Day

> The woman, Folly, is loud; She is undisciplined and without knowledge.
> —*Proverbs 9:13 (author paraphrase)*

Folly—recklessness—stupidity, senselessness, and corruption are not hard to recognize in others. They're actually pretty easy to spot.

We need to surround ourselves with people who aren't afraid to point out the recklessness in our lives.

When we see it, we tend to avoid their sinful ways, just like we avoid loud people if we know the difference between right and wrong. The problem arises when we're the ones who are loud in foolishness and don't realize it. This is why we need to surround ourselves with people who aren't afraid to point out the recklessness in our lives. So, *who do you have* that cares enough about you to tell you when you're being too loud? If you don't have one, find one. . . . they'll probably save your life!

JOURNAL

_____

_____

_____

_____

_____

_____

_____

_____

_____

_____

_____

_____

_____

Day 10

WORDS THAT WOUND AND WORDS THAT HEAL

Have you ever felt like you are walking on eggshells around someone because of the words they use? They hardly ever build anyone up; they more often tear others down, so you never know how to act around them.

Proverb of the Day

The mouth of the righteous is a fountain of life; but violence overwhelms the mouth of the wicked.
—Proverbs 10:11 (author paraphrase)

In this passage, violence isn't referring to the kind we often see in the news.

> *Rarely do healed people hurt people;*
> *healed people heal people!*

Chances are, we've all experienced the pain words can cause. We've all felt the sting of this, so it's mind-blowing that hurtful words even exist; however, hurt people hurt people. If you're still in pain from something someone did to you, pursue the path of forgiveness to walk in righteousness—your language depends on it. Relinquish the hurt so you can be healed! Why? Because rarely do healed people hurt people; healed people heal people!

JOURNAL

_____

_____

_____

_____

_____

_____

_____

_____

_____

_____

_____

Day 11

THE CROSSROADS OF RESPONSE

Has anyone ever spoken ill of you, saying untrue or unkind things? It always brings you to a crossroads on how to respond. You're always given a choice, so what response do you choose?

Proverb of the Day

With their mouths the godless destroys his neighbor, but through knowledge the righteous escape.
—Proverbs 11:9

Those who walk in knowledge understand that listening to remarks that tear you down only causes more issues.

> *The wisdom of Christ is always the key to escape.*

It's even possible that responding to those remarks without wisdom may reinforce a false sense of truth in their accusations. When you come under attack, walk in the ways of Christ, and you will always discover that the accusations lose their power. Often, the words people say about us can feel like a trap, but the wisdom of Christ is always the key to escape. So, obtain knowledge, follow Jesus, and remain free!

JOURNAL

Day 12

WIPE THE LIES FROM YOUR LIPS

Do you enjoy the company of people who lie to you? Of course not. When we discover a liar, most of us struggle to be around them because we know how little they think of us. Their willingness to lie reveals how little they value who we are.

Proverb of the Day

> The LORD detests lying lips, but He delights in those who tell the truth.
>
> —*Proverbs 12:22 (NLT)*

Yes, you read that right; there are things the Lord despises!

No lie is sly enough to keep the truth from God!

The Lord detests a lying character! He wants nothing to do with those who deceive and create confusion, and He definitely won't bless their actions. However, those who are willing to be honest and share the truth in love put a smile on His face. So, the next time you consider lying to save face, just remember that *a lie won't save you* from His! No lie is sly enough to keep the truth from God!

JOURNAL

_____

_____

_____

_____

_____

_____

_____

_____

_____

_____

_____

_____

_____

_____

_____

Day 13

DON'T WASTE THE BLESSINGS

Have you ever seen someone waste something that was given to them? It's unfortunate to see blessings squandered away, and you've probably noticed that doing so cost them.

Proverb of the Day

Whoever scorns instruction will pay for it, but whoever respects a command is rewarded.
—Proverbs 13:13 (NIVUK)

If we can learn to see godly instructions as a blessing, then we can expect to gain. However, when we view them as constricting or oppressive, we'll always disregard them and push through to do it our way.

> *He will take us further than we would ever get on our own.*

But this approach will always cost us. If we can learn that God's ways are better and higher than our own, He will take us further than we would ever get on our own. So, choose to *receive and honor the gift of God's direction every day!*

JOURNAL

_____

_____

_____

_____

_____

_____

_____

_____

_____

_____

_____

_____

_____

_____

Day 14

THE WISDOM TO SHARE

Have you ever known someone who loves to talk about Jesus? When you're with them, the conversation will always turn to Him some way, somehow. In doing so, they help you focus on Him, too!

Proverb of the Day

A truthful witness saves lives, but a false witness is deceitful.

—Proverbs 14:25

We can all be a witness to the goodness of God in our own lives, and our willingness to share His goodness can cause others to embrace it as well.

> *If you're not leading people toward Him, then you're leading them away from Him!*

Proverb 11:30 tells us that a sign of wisdom is the winning of souls. So, the one who shares what God has done in their life is wise! However, the one who doesn't is not only unwise, but they're actually setting themselves up as an enemy of God. If you're not leading people toward Him, then you're leading them away from Him! So, *be wise and share* what the Lord has done!

JOURNAL

_____

_____

_____

_____

_____

_____

_____

_____

_____

_____

_____

_____

_____

Day 15

GUARD YOUR TONGUE

Have you ever stopped to think about how much our words matter? What we say carries weight and can leave long-lasting, and sometimes permanent, effects.

Proverb of the Day

The tongue of the wise adorns knowledge, but the mouth of the fool gushes folly.

—Proverbs 15:2

God tells us that the power of life and death resides in the tongue (Proverbs 18:21). We can use it to speak words that build up or tear down.

> *We should guard our tongues, giving no foothold for Satan to use us as his vessel of delivery.*

As our verse says, someone who uses it to compliment God's knowledge, writings, and way of life operates in His wisdom; however, those who give no thought to what they say are a mouthpiece for the enemy. We should guard our tongues, giving no foothold for Satan to use us as his vessel of delivery. Since God created us, chose us, and celebrates the life He gave us, we should only use words that celebrate Him! So, let's be known as those who *offer words of praise* and bring Him honor!

JOURNAL

_____

_____

_____

_____

_____

_____

_____

_____

_____

_____

Day 16

THE ROAD TO SUCCESS

Have you ever set out to do something but didn't succeed? Did you take the time to reflect on why your plans didn't produce what you were hoping for? Often, when we reflect on the reason for our failures, we discover we tried to go at them alone.

Proverb of the Day

> Commit to the Lord whatever you do, and your plans will succeed. . . . In his heart, a man plans his course, but the Lord determines his steps.
> —Proverbs 16: 3, 9 (author paraphrase)

Both verses speak of a desired destination, a place to reach from where you currently are.

> *Move as He directs!*

Whatever direction you're headed, the thoughts that lead you there should be committed, handed over, and surrendered to God for Him to evaluate. Considering this before you proceed can determine your success! So, take a moment, pause, and talk with God about your plans; then, move as He directs! Now, go and have a successful day!

JOURNAL

_____

_____

_____

_____

_____

_____

_____

_____

_____

_____

_____

_____

_____

_____

Day 17

THE DEATH OF OFFENSE

Have you ever realized how impossible it is to avoid the opportunity for conflict in life? We seem to live in a day and time where everyone is on edge and easily offended. Unfortunately, being offended is a reaction that incites another reaction that causes a cycle of pain to begin.

Proverb of the Day

> *Starting a quarrel is like opening a floodgate, so stop before a dispute breaks out.*
>
> —*Proverbs 17:14 (NLT)*

Consider this: disputes only happen when we negatively respond to someone else's offense.

> *Cover over an offense and promote love!*

The opportunity for a dispute is dead if we choose not to react in offense. They may continue to act out, but the conflict won't survive. Today, let your first response be grace if someone does something to offend you. Don't give a flood of destructive emotions any ground! If this happens, take a moment and place it before God; He'll give you the grace to walk in so that you can live as verse 9 instructs: cover over an offense and promote love!

JOURNAL

_____

_____

_____

_____

_____

_____

_____

_____

_____

_____

_____

Day 18

LISTEN FIRST

Have you ever been around a child who won't listen? Not a disobedient child, but a child who talk-talk-talks. That just shows the energy of a child, but as an adult, it shows our immaturity.

Proverb of the Day

Fools find no pleasure in understanding but delight in airing their own opinions.

—Proverbs 18:2

Many verses in chapter 18 urge us to listen more than we speak and that fools have no interest in listening; they simply enjoy conveying their own thoughts. This unwillingness to close our mouths keeps us a fool because we never have ears to hear, so we can never learn, and the biggest culprit is the "mouth" in our minds!

> *This unwillingness to close our mouths keeps us a fool.*

Too often, we stop listening to what someone else is saying because we've already answered them in our thoughts; we're just waiting for them to stop talking. Today, ask the Lord to show you when you need to listen versus when you need to speak. Who knows, *you may learn something!*

JOURNAL

_____

_____

_____

_____

_____

_____

_____

_____

_____

_____

_____

_____

Day 19

FULLY FULFILLED

Have you ever pondered on a life of fulfillment, especially one void of troubles? Chances are, you have because it's a desire God placed inside all of us.

Proverb of the Day

The fear of the LORD leads to life; then one rests content, untouched by trouble.

—Proverbs 19:23

We all desire to live a life fulfilled, content, and untouched by trouble; however, we may struggle to believe that life is possible because of all we've gone through. But know this: a life overwhelmed by troubles isn't the absence of God, but it very well could signal an absence of the fear of God.

> *Put Him in front of all you do.*

You see, even in the face of trouble, we can live fulfilling lives when we live in awe of the Lord by acknowledging God first in all we do! So, troubles may come, but God's Word says joy comes in the morning (Psalm 30:5). Choose today to live in awe of God, put Him in front of all you do, and watch how fulfilling life can be!

JOURNAL

_____

_____

_____

_____

_____

_____

_____

_____

_____

_____

_____

_____

_____

Day 20

IS IT WORTH IT?

Have you ever wanted to let someone have it, where you just want to tell them off because of what they did and how they made you feel? Would tearing them down build you up?

Proverb of the Day

It is to one's honor to avoid strife, but every fool is quick to quarrel.

—Proverbs 20:3

The verse says that a person who knows how to manage themselves in difficult interpersonal interactions makes deposits in their so-called "honor account." Will the one you lay into honor you?

> *Reserve your anger and preserve your honor.*

Probably not, but then again, it isn't them you need to win over anyway. Instead, reserve your anger and preserve your honor . . .

especially with God! So, before stepping up to stand your ground, step back and see the bigger picture of eternal life—are their actions worth your reputation as a fool?

JOURNAL

_____

_____

_____

_____

_____

_____

_____

_____

_____

_____

_____

_____

_____

_____

_____

Day 21

OBEDIENCE OVER OFFERING

Have you ever felt the need to sacrifice something because of a wrong you did? We often feel the urge to right our wrongs. However, God has a different idea for us.

Proverb of the Day

> The LORD is more pleased when we do what is right and just than when we offer Him sacrifices.
> —Proverbs 21:3 (NLT)

Throughout the Bible, people offered sacrifices to make up for their wrongs.

> *Obedience is the true sign of remorse and repentance.*

While sacrifice was a valuable part of life, God greatly desired a return to obedience. Why? Because sacrifice is like receiving an apology from someone who did something on purpose. Could they be sorry for their wrongs? Possibly, but chances are, they're apologizing to cover themselves. Instead, obedience is the true sign of remorse and repentance. Our obedience shows God that we acknowledge our wrongs, trust that He is right, and want to *follow His ways.*

JOURNAL

_____

_____

_____

_____

_____

_____

_____

_____

_____

_____

_____

_____

_____

_____

Day 22

THE LION IS NO EXCUSE

Have you ever made excuses to avoid doing something you know you should do? We all do it, and sometimes, the excuse is valid, but most of the time, it's nothing more than an exaggerated explanation as to why we don't do what we should do.

Proverb of the Day

> The slacker says, "There is a lion outside! I will be slain in the streets!"
>
> —Proverbs 22:13 (BSB)

The writer of this proverb shows us that our excuses are not always rooted in reality! Was there a lion outside? Probably not, but we often make these excuses to avoid doing what even God has called us to do.

> *Would I rather make progress by trusting in God or remain where I am in dishonor?*

While our excuses may make us feel better, they don't change God's mind; they just make us look dishonorable. So, the question we have to ask ourselves is this: Would I rather make progress by trusting in God or remain where I am in dishonor? Please know that *God is with us* and will help us overcome our fear, even the "lion" we tell ourselves is outside.

JOURNAL

_____

_____

_____

_____

_____

_____

_____

_____

_____

_____

_____

_____

_____

Day 23

TO INVEST OR NOT TO INVEST

Have you ever observed someone's actions and realized you had advice that could benefit their life? How did you decide whether to give it or not? We should consider the information we have as valuable so that it's not wasted.

Proverb of the Day

Don't try to talk sense to a fool; he can't appreciate it.
—Proverbs 23:9 (GNT)

Each day, we come across people we would love to invest in with our wisdom, but we need to weigh the cost. Why? Our wisdom is a blessing from God, and God intends us to steward it.

> *If you want to gain wisdom to offer wisdom, don't be a fool with what God has given you!*

To steward is to be responsible for managing and caring for what has been entrusted to you. Offering wisdom to someone who won't receive it but actually abuses it is to waste what God has given you. Before you share your words of wisdom with someone today, first, weigh the cost of investment—will it produce a return, or will it go unnoticed and be wasted? If you want to gain wisdom to offer wisdom, don't be a fool with what God has given you!

JOURNAL

_____

_____

_____

_____

_____

_____

_____

_____

_____

_____

_____

Day 24

RESISTING REVENGE

Have you ever heard of the "Golden Rule": Do unto others as you would have them do unto you? Chances are you have, especially as a child, when a kid took something of yours and you reacted in anger.

Proverb of the Day

Do not say. "I'll do to them as they have done to me; I'll pay them back for what they did."
—Proverbs 24:29

When someone has done something to you, be cautious of misleading emotions to retaliate—even if you have the right to.

> *That's your character; protect it!*

Emotions driving the need for revenge will bring out the worst in us and cause us to lose sight of our godly character, ultimately stealing our witness as followers of Christ. So, don't allow a vengeful reaction to give someone permission to attack your character today! That's your character; protect it! Remember, we're called to be a witness to God's kindness in the same way Jesus responded to us when we attacked Him!

JOURNAL

_____

_____

_____

_____

_____

_____

_____

_____

_____

_____

_____

_____

_____

_____

Day 25

SPIRITUAL CONTAMINATION

Have you ever picked up a glass of water for a drink, only to discover it was dirty? Although it could quench your thirst, do you desire dirty water? Chances are, you don't!

Proverb of the Day

Like a muddied spring or a polluted well are the righteous who give way to the wicked.

—Proverbs 25:26

Someone who claims to be a follower of Jesus but allows the ways of the world to contaminate their life can't quench God's thirst to spread His Good News.

> *Avoid life's contaminants by walking in His ways and remaining useful for His purpose!*

In Revelation 3, Jesus told the church that their efforts looked right, but unfortunately, they were useless to Him. He compared their actions to lukewarm water, something worth nothing because water like this was considered dirty and contaminated. He tells them He will spit them out if they don't change. So, avoid life's contaminants by walking in His ways and remaining useful for His purpose!

JOURNAL

_____

_____

_____

_____

_____

_____

_____

_____

_____

_____

_____

_____

Day 26

COMBATING THE CURSE

Has someone ever spoken a word—or what felt like a curse—over you that you didn't deserve? It probably attacked your mind, causing all kinds of doubt to settle in and knock you off your course.

Proverb of the Day

> *Like a fluttering sparrow or a darting swallow, an undeserved curse will not land on its intended victim.*
> —*Proverbs 26:2 (NLT)*

One of the most dangerous things we can do when a curse is spoken over us is to believe it and speak it over ourselves.

> *I am who God says I am!*

Although someone else's words are effective in bringing us down, none is more effective than our own. If you ever find yourself in that place, take hold of these declarations:

I am the head and not the tail! I am above and not beneath! My God goes before me, preparing a way; He has covered the path that follows me! I am not what this world says about me; I am who God says I am! AMEN! Lean into what He says through His Word, and let the undeserved curse flutter away!

JOURNAL

_____

_____

_____

_____

_____

_____

_____

_____

_____

_____

_____

_____

Day 27

WHO ARE YOU REFLECTING?

Have you ever thought about who you surround yourself with? Have you considered their characteristics and how you may reflect them? It is essential to keep an eye on how others influence us because we tend to take on the image of those we're with the most.

Proverb of the Day

As a face is reflected in water, so the heart reflects the real person.

—*Proverbs 27:19 (NLT)*

Those we surround ourselves with have characteristics that influence the core of who we are.

> *Are you close enough to Jesus that you've taken on His characteristics and reflect them?*

Often, *heart* is a figurative word in the Bible that refers to our core, and just as water will reflect our face, our heart reflects the people we're closest to. With this understanding, we should ask ourselves: Who am I surrounding myself with? Then, consider if their character is pleasing to the Lord to help you determine whether they should be in your life. But the BIG question is this: Are you close enough to Jesus that you've taken on His characteristics and reflect them? If we're to look like anyone, it should , be Him!

JOURNAL

_____

_____

_____

_____

_____

_____

_____

_____

_____

_____

_____

Day 28

ARE YOU LISTENING?

Have you ever met a fool? You'd probably say yes if you knew that a fool is someone who won't receive advice. Today, society is full of people with advice to give but seemingly empty of those willing to receive it. Now the question is: Have you ever been the fool?

Proverb of the Day

If you think you know it all, you're a fool for sure; real survivors learn wisdom from others.
                              —*Proverbs 28:26 (MSG)*

Wisdom, knowledge, and understanding come from the hands of those willing to offer it and are gained by those willing to receive it.

> *We should be mature enough to listen so we can survive!*

We should ask ourselves: Am I open to receiving advice, or do I tend to greet advice with an excuse? When someone who reflects the life of Christ offers us advice, we should be willing to listen, receive, consider, and take time to pray about what they have shared. We shouldn't be quick to excuse what someone else offers us; we should be mature enough to listen so we can survive!

JOURNAL

_____

_____

_____

_____

_____

_____

_____

_____

_____

_____

_____

_____

_____

_____

Day 29

EMOTION MANAGEMENT

Have you ever considered just how powerful our emotions are—what they create inside of us, what they cause us to do, and how they affect others? Emotions are a wonderful thing to have; God Himself created and has them, but they can be just as devastating when not guarded.

Proverb of the Day

> A fool gives full vent to his anger, but a wise man keeps himself under control.
>
> —Proverbs 29:11 (author paraphrase)

From this verse, you can see that anger isn't a problem but becomes one when it's not managed and fully vented—expressed or released without holding back.

> *We're not in control of theirs;*
> *we're only in control of ours.*

Expressing anger isn't bad, but it must be handled wisely so that it doesn't handle us! When our emotions come under attack because of someone else's actions, we should take a moment to consider grace—for them and for us. Their emotions may show their lack of grace for us, but we're not in control of theirs; we're only in control of ours. We must *ask the Holy Spirit to help* us guard our emotions and manage them accordingly so we don't become the fool.

JOURNAL

Day 30

CERTAINTY IN UNCERTAINTY

Have you ever experienced absolute certainty before? Certainty breeds comfort, gives us peace of mind, and strengthens our confidence. Think of a time you found yourself in an uncertain situation. If you'll remember, all you desired was to anchor to something that would settle the chaos in your mind.

Proverb of the Day

Every word of God is flawless; He is a shield to those who take refuge in Him.

—Proverbs 30:5

God's Word can anchor us in times of uncertainty because that's Who He is; He is an anchor to our souls: our mind, will, and emotions.

> *His words are our refuge!*

Hebrews 6:18 tells us that God has given both His promise and His oath; they're unchangeable and a place of refuge for those needing hope. When we face unsettling situations and feel like we're being tossed back and forth in our emotions, we should take hold of God's Word—He's promised to be our shield against these attacks— Let's enter into His presence; His words are our refuge!

JOURNAL

_____

_____

_____

_____

_____

_____

_____

_____

_____

_____

_____

_____

_____

_____

_____

Day 31

A STEWARD OF INFLUENCE

Have you ever realized how our influence can bless others when we steward it well? We constantly influence others whether we want to or not. We have no control over that, but we do have control over what our influence looks like.

Proverb of the Day

> *It is not for kings, Lemuel–it is not for kings to drink wine, not for rulers to crave beer.*
>
> —Proverbs 31:4

This advice comes from a mother caring for her son. She knew his position would be in jeopardy if he involved himself in things that could negatively affect his influence.

> *God's reputation is more valuable than anything we enjoy!*

Every day, we need to consider our position in the eyes of others and whether there are things, public or private, that could damage our influence. We may even feel we have a right to certain things, but they must go if they could jeopardize our impact for His glory. We must decide that God's reputation is more valuable than anything we enjoy! We may not be kings, but God has given us influence, and we should guard it!

JOURNAL

Day 32

RATE YOUR REVERENCE

Have you ever missed out on something valuable because you didn't cherish it enough to participate? It's a frustrating place to be because we look back and wonder what might have been.

Proverb of the Day

> *The fear of the LORD is the beginning of knowledge, but fools despise wisdom and instruction.*
>
> —*Proverbs 1:7*

Let's take a moment and rate our reverence for God on a scale of 1-10. How did you rate yourself?

> *The best way for us to gain this reverence is to spend time getting to know Him.*

Chances are, we all probably rated it higher than it actually is. So, how do we arrive at the correct score? By the wisdom we live out according to His Word. Simply put, reverence produces wisdom. However, genuine reverence will only come when we have a healthy awareness of who He is, and the best way for us to gain this reverence is to spend time getting to know Him. Let's not be fools; let's be wise enough to cherish time with God and *create moments* throughout our day where we pause and get to know Him!

JOURNAL

_____

_____

_____

_____

_____

_____

_____

_____

_____

_____

_____

_____

_____

Day 33

WHAT PATH ARE YOU ON?

Have you ever followed someone because you were unsure where you were going or what was ahead, and as you followed, you kept your head down and missed their guidance?

Proverb of the Day

He holds victory in store for the upright, He is a shield to those whose walk is blameless, for He guards the course of the just and protects the way of His faithful ones.
—Proverbs 2:7-8

It's such a blessing to have a God who desires to go before us.

> *He only promises victory for those who follow Him there!*

We need to understand that things may not be as we want them to be, but they'll always be as they need to be when we follow Him. We should all be aware that when we allow our wants to outweigh His ways, we find ourselves outside His protection. Every day, we choose to follow Him in His ways or lead ourselves in our own; the choice is ours to make. But remember, He only promises victory for those who follow Him there! So, as we go throughout our day, we should *look up* and ensure we're following Him and haven't wandered onto our own path!

JOURNAL

Day 34

DON'T DREAD DISCIPLINE

Have you ever been corrected before? Better yet, did you make room for the correction because you knew you deserved or needed it? It's hardly ever enjoyable to receive, but whether it's enjoyable doesn't determine whether it's beneficial.

Proverb of the Day

> *My child, don't reject the LORD's discipline, and don't be upset when He corrects you.*
>
> —*Proverbs 3:11 (NLT)*

As followers of Christ, we will experience the Lord's discipline many times throughout our lives!

> *Being childlike isn't bad, but being childish is an issue.*

Sometimes we listen, sometimes we don't; it all depends on how much we agree with His direction. However, our willingness to receive the correction that only we approve is childish and proves we need discipline. Yes, a full-grown adult can be childish. Being childlike isn't bad, but being child*ish* is an issue . . . and ignoring corrections? Well, that's childish! So, the next time we sense our Heavenly Father correcting us, we should realize the heart behind it and pause to say thank you. He's simply trying to show us, His children, that *there's a better way* to live!

JOURNAL

_____

_____

_____

_____

_____

_____

_____

_____

_____

_____

_____

_____

Day 35

GUARD YOUR HEART

Have you ever been given the responsibility to guard something? How about something so important that your life depended on it? If your life depends on it, then whatever you're guarding is of great value. So, the level at which we guard something is determined by the value we place on it.

Proverb of the Day

> Above all else, guard your heart, for everything you do flows from it.
>
> —Proverbs 4:23

Our hearts are often unaware of the dangers lurking around us; therefore, they require heavy guarding.

He desires to guard us because He values us!

The heart represents the core of who we are and what our life flows through. When our hearts are unguarded, emotions can easily drive our lives and lead us down a dangerous path. The best way to guard against this is by daily inviting Jesus into our lives. Every day, we need to give Him room to come in and guard our hearts so that the emotions of life won't drive us! Let's put Jesus at the core of every decision we make; He desires to guard us because He values us!

JOURNAL

_____

_____

_____

_____

_____

_____

_____

_____

_____

_____

_____

_____

Day 36

LOVE BEYOND OUR SIN

Have you ever known something about someone, but they acted as if you had no clue? No matter how much you tried to address it, they just kept sticking their heads in the sand and pretending you couldn't see it.

Proverb of the Day

For your ways are in full view of the LORD, and He examines all your paths.

—Proverbs 5:21

We must realize that God still knows our sins even in our best attempts to hide them from Him. There's nothing He doesn't see!

> ## His love outweighs our rejection!

However, not only does He see what we're doing and the path that led us there, but He also sees the pathway out. It's wonderful news that our detours away from Him don't deter Him away from us;

His love for us is that great! Even when we insult Him by sticking our heads in the sand, His love outweighs our rejection! He still desires to offer us a way out! So, let's stop hiding from Him and start talking to Him!

JOURNAL

_____

_____

_____

_____

_____

_____

_____

_____

_____

_____

_____

_____

_____

_____

Day 37

THE DANGERS OF DIVISION

Have you ever disrupted someone's journey? No matter how small or life-altering, you did something that changed their course.

Proverb of the Day

> *There are six things the Lord hates, seven that are detestable to Him: . . . a man who stirs up dissension among brothers.*
>
> —*Proverbs 6:16, 19 (author paraphrase)*

Dissension is disruption of the greatest kind.

> *Ask Him to give you the wisdom and strength to go and repair the damage you've done.*

Someone who sows discord between people who have previously worked together can be detrimental to the outcome of what they set out to do, and when this happens within the body of Christ, God views it with passionate disdain. Isn't this a fair response? How would we feel if someone brought dissension to our family and divided us against one another? We wouldn't like it either! Without consideration, that person would now be your enemy! If, by chance, you have caused dissension with God's people, first, ask God for forgiveness, then ask Him to give you the wisdom and strength to go and repair the damage you've done. It may be hard and unnerving to revisit, but fixing the course is worth it!

JOURNAL

Day 38

STAY AWAY FROM THE LINE!

Have you ever flirted with sin? Maybe you never acted on it, but it was within your reach, ready for you to grasp. The temptation may have already captured your attention and fueled your desire, but how close are you to the line?

Proverb of the Day

> My son, keep my words and store up my commands within you. Keep my commands and you will live; guard my teachings as the apple of your eye.
>
> —Proverbs 7:1-2

Often, we find ourselves in a tug-of-war between two decisions: what we know and what we desire.

What line am I too close to because I'm not close enough to the wisdom of God?

We need to realize that in this world, something will always try to arrest our attention, so we must keep God's Word at the forefront in our lives to recognize the snare. However, the best thing to do is gain so much of His wisdom that we avoid the line of sin altogether. Ultimately, we must avoid giving the line of sin attention if we want to avoid flirting with it and crossing over it! What line am I too close to because I'm not close enough to the wisdom of God?

JOURNAL

_____

_____

_____

_____

_____

_____

_____

_____

_____

_____

_____

Day 39

WALKING WITH WISDOM

Have you ever observed how you pursue wisdom? Is it something grabbed hold of as needed, or something always present leading every decision? Wisdom is something first considered or an afterthought, but either way, it will always reveal itself.

Proverb of the Day

> *I [Wisdom] love those who love me, and those who seek me find me.*
> —*Proverbs 8:17 (author addition)*

Wisdom is intended to be sought out, found, and embraced. Wisdom was never designed to be a tool you grab when you need it; instead, it should be a resource that's always present.

> *We can live without it, but we won't ever have life without it!*

We should cherish God's wisdom as a gift at all times! Consider this: what God created first and used to craft all of creation is available for us to walk through life with. Wisdom is important, and life isn't possible without it. Sure, we can live without it, but we won't ever *have* life without it! Just as God brought forth wisdom before anything in creation took place, we should learn from His ways and *bring forth His wisdom* in our lives before we act.

JOURNAL

Day 40

THE CORRECTION TEST

Have you ever attempted to correct someone, for them only to become upset with you? You saw something that needed addressing, but your effort was met with resistance and rejection.

Proverb of the Day

Whoever corrects a mocker invites insults; whoever rebukes the wicked incurs abuse.

—Proverbs 9:7

Why does God communicate this? He knows we waste our breath on someone who doesn't listen to correction. Not only do we waste our breath, but we also have to deal with their backlash.

> ## *How do you receive correction?*

Now, let's look at ourselves. When someone corrects us, are we wasting their time, or are we receiving it as an opportunity for growth? The passage goes on to say, If you correct those who care about life, they'll love you for it (v. 8). So, how do you receive correction? As one who loves life or loves being right? How we receive correction tells God, others, and even ourselves a lot about what kind of person we are. We should all take some time to reflect on how we respond to corrections to ensure we *continue to receive them!*

JOURNAL

_____

_____

_____

_____

_____

_____

_____

_____

_____

_____

_____

_____

_____

_____

Day 41

THE CHOICES THAT CROWN US

Have you ever felt torn between two very important life choices? What do I choose—this or that? We must weigh these out because our decisions in life matter!

Proverb of the Day

Blessings crown the head of the righteous.

—*Proverbs 10:6*

Choices matter because they speak to our character and identity.

> *Our choices matter.*

Our verse says that God's blessings will be on us when our decisions are made according to His ways. It also says His favor will be offered as a crown. Crowns are an indication of power and authority. So, His favor is placed on us to acknowledge His power and authority are with us. But it doesn't stop there; it says that this indication of favor is placed on our heads, signifying that it's to be seen, but seen for the glory of the One who offers it. Our decisions of righteousness mark us with the testimony of God's goodness so others will be drawn to make righteous decisions in their lives. Our choices matter, so let's make sure our decisions crown us with God's favor to point others toward Him!

JOURNAL

Day 42

IDENTIFYING WISDOM IN ACTION

Have you ever considered what wise actions look like? They must look a certain way to be recognized; the judgment can't be subjective. Wise actions produce fruit that comes from an absolute truth, so what does it look like?

Proverb of the Day

The fruit of the righteous is a tree of life, And he who wins souls is wise.

—Proverbs 11:30 (NKJV)

The most incredible display of wisdom is producing fruit that leads others to Christ! Nothing is closer to the heart of our Father in Heaven than that!

There is nothing like living a life to see the lost saved!

Don't get me wrong; there are many significant indicators regarding wisdom: how you spend your money, use your tongue, control your temper, and so many more, but there is none like living a life to see the lost saved! We can all evaluate our wisdom by our efforts to reach others for Christ. So, how does your wisdom look? *Is it noticeable?*

JOURNAL

_____

_____

_____

_____

_____

_____

_____

_____

_____

_____

_____

_____

_____

Day 43

LIVING TO PLEASE THE GROOM

Have you ever thought about your role in representing the bride of Christ? Do you consider how she presents? Now, take a moment and imagine what she may look like from the Groom's point of view.

Proverb of the Day

A wife of noble character is her husband's crown, but a disgraceful wife is like decay to his bones.
—Proverbs 12:4

Something of noble character is stainless and spotless.

> *We're a crown worth wearing!*

Imagine if a bride focused all her attention on how her husband sees her instead of how she or anyone else sees her. How much more pleasing would that be to her groom? Too often, we get so distracted by the way we present ourselves to everyone else, or even to ourselves, that we forget that the only One that matters is the One we will be with for all of eternity. So, let's choose to live in such a way that puts a smile on Christ's face because we're a crown worth wearing!

JOURNAL

_____

_____

_____

_____

_____

_____

_____

_____

_____

_____

_____

_____

_____

_____

Day 44

THE BUSINESS OF WORDS

Have you ever thought of your words as workers that build up or tear down? Every day, we speak words that work on our behalf; the question is, what are they up to?

Proverb of the Day

> *Those who guard their lips preserve their lives, but those who speak rashly will come to ruin.*
>
> *—Proverbs 13:3*

The words we deploy matter because they either help us or hurt us. The great news is that we choose what words go to work and what words get fired! And let's be honest, we all have words that need to be fired . . . AMEN!

> *Opening your mouth can ruin everything.*

Some words we use or say have been around for too long, but just like business, length of employment doesn't equal quality of work! If they're not building, then it's time for them to get corrected or get gone! The NLT translates the last part of the verse like this: opening your mouth can ruin everything. So, *let's decide* what we want our words to do before we open up for business!

JOURNAL

_____

_____

_____

_____

_____

_____

_____

_____

_____

_____

_____

_____

_____

_____

Day 45

TRUST THE GPS

Have you ever gone on a trip without directions, driving to your destination based on instinct alone? Probably not. Most of us allow the expertise of a GPS to set the course for our desired destination, especially if we've never been there.

Proverb of the Day

> There is a way that appears to be right, but in the end it leads to death.
>
> —Proverbs 14:12

Every day, we travel toward a destination we've never been to: heaven. Along this journey, we need guidance because the occasional Sunday direction won't work.

> *Without His help, we won't reach where we intend to go.*

Our pride tells us we can arrive at our destination with minimal advice, but only One knows the way, and that's Jesus Christ! Jesus offers us the directions we need through His Word, and His Spirit provides the expertise to navigate them; without His help, we won't reach where we intend to go. It's time to let go of our pride, *receive the direction,* and arrive at the desired destination.

JOURNAL

_____

_____

_____

_____

_____

_____

_____

_____

_____

_____

_____

_____

_____

Day 46

GIVE LIFE TO OTHERS

Has an encouraging word from someone ever made your day? It feels good, doesn't it? It feels good when we encourage others, too. But why? Because God made us to give and receive life through our interactions with others.

Proverb of the Day

> *A cheerful look brings joy to the heart; good news gives health to the bones.*
> —*Proverbs 15:30 (author paraphrase)*

Encouraging words, such as acknowledging someone's value, strengthens them to the core. Their faith in the foundation that holds them up gets stronger and healthier, which means we're helping them last longer. And guess what? The same goes for us!

Let's consider our interactions to give and receive life for God's glory!

We should not only strive to help people become healthier and stronger in spirit, but we should also surround ourselves with those who do the same for us. If God tells us that encouraging a person strengthens and enhances us, then He also tells us that being around people who don't do this weakens and diminishes us. So, we should choose who we surround ourselves with wisely! As we go through our day, let's consider our interactions to give and receive life for God's glory!

JOURNAL

_____

_____

_____

_____

_____

_____

_____

_____

_____

_____

_____

Day 47

DON'T TAKE THAT EXIT

Have you ever driven on the interstate through a major city? If so, you may have noticed that you ride above the city streets as you pass through. In most cities, it is dangerous to take the wrong exit into a bad area because of possible crime. However, staying on the highway and passing those dangerous areas significantly diminishes your chances of encountering crime.

Proverb of the Day

The highway of the upright avoids evil; those who guard his way guard his life.
—Proverbs 16:17 (author paraphrase)

We need to be aware of what lies beneath so we can avoid exiting safe areas and entering unsafe areas—areas that subject us to things that aren't pleasing to God.

He'll ensure you arrive safely!

I'm sure you know what those areas are for you! Just as we avoid the wrong exits when we travel, we must avoid taking exits that expose us to danger and cause us to drift. Before you go about your day today, take time and ask God what areas you should avoid. He'll ensure you arrive safely!

JOURNAL

_____

_____

_____

_____

_____

_____

_____

_____

_____

_____

_____

_____

Day 48

GIVE WHAT WE'VE BEEN GIVEN

Have you ever chosen not to respond in offense, even though, by all measures, you had a right to? You may have known that being offended comes with great responsibility.

Proverb of the Day

> *He who covers over an offense promotes love, but whoever repeats the matter separates close friends.*
> *—Proverbs 17:9 (author paraphrase)*

When someone launches an offense at us, we have the power to decide where things go from there—we can either expose the offense or cover it.

> *He didn't respond according to what we deserved; He responded according to what was best.*

Some translations use the word conceals in place of covers. Both words suggest that a person who promotes love absorbs the offense instead of returning it to the other person, which is exactly what God did for us through Jesus Christ. Through Jesus, God absorbed our offense to promote love and protect the relationship. Think about it: our offense broke the relationship; God's absorption fixed it! He didn't respond according to what we deserved; He responded according to what was best. Let's choose to *offer what we've been given* the next time someone offends us.

JOURNAL

_____

_____

_____

_____

_____

_____

_____

_____

_____

_____

_____

Day 49

WHO'S GOT YOU COVERED?

Have you ever felt unsafe and uncertain? As frightened as we may be, we often put on a strong face to try and overshadow our fear, but let's be honest, it's nothing more than a facade.

Proverb of the Day

> The name of the LORD is a fortified tower; the righteous run to it and are safe.
>
> —Proverbs 18:10

Putting on a strong face and pretending all is well in the face of adversity is a sin because we're choosing to cover ourselves instead of allowing God to cover us.

> *The righteous consider no one else than Jesus!*

Those in right standing don't just mosey over to Jesus when it's convenient as if He's the last resort; no, they take off in a dead sprint and run to His Name! The righteous consider no one else than Jesus! When we face challenges, let's remain under the covering of His Name rather than try to cover ourselves—let's *step into His strength* and let Him take care of us!

JOURNAL

_____

_____

_____

_____

_____

_____

_____

_____

_____

_____

_____

_____

_____

Day 50

DON'T SWEAT IT!

Have you ever lent money to someone knowing you may not receive a reward? You probably felt relieved if you saw a return on your money!

Proverb of the Day

Whoever is kind to the poor lends to the LORD, and he will reward them for what they have done.

—*Proverbs 19:17*

This verse isn't just about money, although we can use money to express kindness; however, this verse refers to the kindness salvation offers! And as we extend this kindness to others, we don't have to sweat whether they can repay it; God guarantees the return on their behalf!

We don't have to sweat the return; God guarantees it!

It may feel risky because the other person doesn't deserve it, but God isn't in the business of lending to those who deserve it, and neither should we! If we want to receive the greatest return anyone can ever gain, then lending God's kindness through Jesus Christ is our investment. Remember, we don't have to sweat the return; God guarantees it!

JOURNAL

_____

_____

_____

_____

_____

_____

_____

_____

_____

_____

_____

_____

Day 51

MORE THAN A CLAIM

Have you ever missed out on something because you didn't believe in it enough? Sometimes, it's no big deal, but other times, it's life-altering!

Proverb of the Day

> Many claim to have unfailing love, but a faithful person who can find?
>
> —*Proverbs 20:6*

God makes such an eye-opening statement in His Word that should cause us to evaluate every step we take. The statement is this: "Not everyone who says to Me, 'Lord, Lord,' will enter the Kingdom of Heaven, but only *the one* who does the will of My Father" (Matthew 7:21).

> *He's looking for those who have the faith to live it out!*

In this passage, Jesus says that only a few will find their way. Sadly, this has been the story throughout the history of mankind when it comes to God's desire to save His people; few were saved in the flood, few entered the Promise Land, and few chose to become followers of Christ. God is looking for more than a claim; He's looking for those who have the faith to live it out! God has invited us to join Him; let's not miss out!

JOURNAL

_____

_____

_____

_____

_____

_____

_____

_____

_____

_____

_____

Day 52

THE SACRIFICE OF GENEROSITY

Have you ever found yourself considering your wants and needs over that of another person? It's not hard to do, but we must realize that we've lost sight of generosity the moment we consider ourselves first.

Proverb of the Day

The righteous give without sparing.

—Proverbs 21:26

Generosity is measured by our willingness to sacrifice ourselves for the benefit of others. Generosity isn't just about kindness; true generosity will cost us something.

He has called us to live out the standard that He has set!

The root word for generous is genre, a Latin word meaning to birth, produce, or create. Generosity through the lens of this verse means that when we give without sparing, we birth, produce, or create something in the one who receives it—this is what God did for us! Because He gave and sacrificed Himself, His generosity has given us life! He has called us to live out the standard that He has set! As we choose to live in right standing with God, we should *look for opportunities* to give life to others.

JOURNAL

_____

_____

_____

_____

_____

_____

_____

_____

_____

_____

Day 53

THE SHADOW OF REPUTATION

Have you ever looked at your life through someone else's eyes? It can be sobering because our reputation—how we're seen in the eyes of others—is very revealing.

Proverb of the Day

> *A good name is more desirable than great riches; to be esteemed is better than silver or gold.*
> —*Proverbs 22:1*

Abraham Lincoln said, "Character is like a tree, and reputation is like its shadow. The shadow is what we think of it; the tree is the real thing."

> *Every day, we must consider the shadow we cast; the value of our influence depends on it.*

The shadow we cast is often all that people ever see, and this shadow determines our reputation, so how we act matters. We must also remember that the way one person sees us is often the way other people see us—reputations spread like wildfires. Our reputation may not be who we are, but we may never get the chance to prove it. As ambassadors for Christ, our reputation opens or closes the door to doing our job. Every day, we must consider the shadow we cast; the value of our influence depends on it.

JOURNAL

Day 54

MAKE HIM SMILE

Have you ever put a smile on someone's face? It feels good, doesn't it? Making someone smile makes you smile, too. A smile is an external expression of internal joy. The simple gestures we offer to put a smile on someone's face go a long way in producing life in them and in us!

Proverb of the Day

My son, if your heart is wise, then My heart will be glad indeed; My inmost being will rejoice when your lips speak what is right.

—Proverbs 23:15

The Bible tells us that out of the heart, the mouth speaks and that good things come from the good in our hearts (Luke 6:45).

> *Let's choose to fill up so*
> *we can pour out.*

In our proverb of the day, God is encouraging us to put a smile on His face by allowing the wisdom He has given us to pass through our lips to encourage others. However, this all starts with our willingness to gain His wisdom. So, every day, let's choose to fill up so we can pour out; only then can we end our day knowing we *put a smile on His face*—because we gave life to someone else!

JOURNAL

_____

_____

_____

_____

_____

_____

_____

_____

_____

_____

_____

_____

Day 55

UNBLISSFUL IGNORANCE

Have you ever bought into the saying, "Ignorance is bliss?" This phrase simply means *if I don't know about it, then* it's not my issue. While it sounds very freeing, is it how God desires for us to live?

Proverb of the Day

> Rescue those who are unjustly sentenced to die; save them as they stagger to their death. Don't excuse yourself by saying, "Look, we didn't know." For God understands all hearts, and he sees you. He who guards your heart knows you knew. He will repay all people as their actions deserve.
>
> —Proverbs 24:11-12 (NLT)

So, is ignorance bliss? Only if bliss means God's repayment to us for ignoring the lost and focusing on self.

Plowing through life for our own desires leads us away from Him.

It's too easy to get so consumed with our busyness that we forget to look up and see those staggering toward death. However, living with our heads down and plowing through life for our own desires leads us away from Him, too. Let's choose to *look up*, see others, and do our best to help rescue those headed toward their end!

JOURNAL

_____

_____

_____

_____

_____

_____

_____

_____

_____

_____

_____

_____

_____

Day 56

HEAP COALS ON THEIR HEADS

Have you ever noticed how easy it is to attack someone who's attacking you? However, when we attack back, their actions become the actions we embrace.

Proverb of the Day

If your enemy is hungry, give them food to eat; if he is thirsty, give him water to drink. In doing this, you will heap burning coals on his head, and the LORD will reward you.
—*Proverbs 25:21-22*

It is standard practice in battle to look for your opponent's weaknesses and attack them. However, this verse encourages us to look for their weakness and help them.

> *He doesn't retaliate by causing us pain;*
> *He purifies us by offering us help.*

We're encouraged to care for our enemies by purifying their hearts—that's what coal and fire do; they purify. When we act in ways that attack God, He doesn't retaliate by causing us pain; He purifies us by offering us help. God's heart for us is redemption because He desires that no one should perish (2 Peter 3:9), no matter how severely someone attacks Him. So, the next time we come under attack, let's offer to *help instead of harm!*

JOURNAL

_____

_____

_____

_____

_____

_____

_____

_____

_____

_____

_____

_____

_____

_____

Day 57

THE REAL DEAL

Have you ever bought something faux, imitation, counterfeit, phony, false, sham, or fake? These are all words that describe something of lesser value or desire. However, we are all looking for something that is truly valuable—the real thing, not something pretending to be something else.

Proverb of the Day

> Smooth words may hide a wicked heart, just as a pretty glaze covers a clay pot.
>
> —Proverbs 26:23 (NLT)

Yes, sometimes we're okay with saving some money on that "Folex" or "Louis Fuitton," but when it comes to a friend, we're looking for the real deal.

> *Relationships cost us something, and buying into a fake one will cost us more than we're ready to spend!*

We must be careful of people who present well but have the wrong motives. Relationships cost us something, and buying into a fake one will cost us more than we're ready to spend! We need to allow the Holy Spirit to guide us in the relationships we form. So, let's allow our Best Friend to lead us to real friends and save us from an unfortunate expense!

JOURNAL

_____

_____

_____

_____

_____

_____

_____

_____

_____

_____

_____

_____

Day 58

TODAY'S BLESSINGS

Have you ever considered how the future can steal your present? It's not hard to get so caught up in what's to come that we forget about what's happening right now.

Proverb of the Day

> *Don't brag about tomorrow, since you don't know what the day will bring.*
>
> *—Proverbs 27:1 (NLT)*

When we focus on our tomorrow, we lose sight of what we have today. Yes, what lies ahead could be great, exciting, and desirable, but we can't forget to be grateful for today's blessings.

> *Focus on today so you don't get too distracted by tomorrow.*

If we don't learn to be present, then we'll also overlook the thing we are waiting for. Daily, we should consider what God has blessed us with and what we have to be thankful for. There's always something; chances are, there are many things, and if it's a person, tell them! Being grateful for what we have honors God because His Word says every good and perfect gift *is* from above (James 1:17). So, remember to focus on today so you don't get too distracted by tomorrow.

JOURNAL

_____

_____

_____

_____

_____

_____

_____

_____

_____

_____

_____

_____

Day 59

THE DOOR TO HIS FAITHFULNESS

Have you ever thought about our obedience in relation to God's faithfulness? Faithful is who He is, but our obedience opens the door to experiencing it.

Proverb of the Day

If anyone turns a deaf ear to my instruction, even their prayers are detestable.

—Proverbs 28:9

Obedience to His way of life matters!

> *We need to understand that our obedience opens the door for our prayers to be received.*

Our willingness to follow His instructions opens the door to His blessing and prosperity (Deuteronomy 28:1-4), protection and guidance (Psalm 119:105-106), favor with Him and man (Proverbs

3:1-4), health and nourishment (Proverbs 3:7-8), joy and peace (John 15:10-11), and most importantly, eternal life (Hebrews 5:9). Most of the prayers we pray fall into one of these categories. We need to understand that our obedience opens the door for our prayers to be received. God has given us His instructions; let's follow them and experience the faithful relationship He offers us. If we desire for God to hear us, we must desire to walk in His ways!

JOURNAL

_____

_____

_____

_____

_____

_____

_____

_____

_____

_____

_____

_____

Day 60

IN A WORLD FULL OF MOCKERS

Have you ever been in a volatile situation with someone? Whether with our spouse, kids, parents, or co-workers, you name it, relationships host an opportunity for emotions to escalate and cause damage. However, they also host the opportunity to calm emotions and offer healing.

Proverb of the Day

Mockers stir up a city, but the wise turn away anger.
—Proverbs 29:8

We've all met that person who enrages others with their words or actions. The NASB translation uses the word "arrogant"—someone who is condescendingly self-satisfied—instead of "mocker." This means they make everything about themselves, no matter the damage they cause.

> *Mockers may stir things up, but we can be wise and calm things down.*

If you've ever been around an arrogant person, you know they know how to get under the skin. When we encounter someone like this, we shouldn't give them our attention; we should give it to those they affected. Mockers may stir things up, but we can be wise and calm things down. This doesn't mean we confront the mocker; the Bible is clear on not addressing fools. Instead, we turn our attention to those affected in hopes of bringing them peace; this is what Jesus did with the adulterous woman. Today, if you see a situation going sideways because of someone's actions, step in, but as one who helps care for those affected, to bring peace!

JOURNAL

_____

_____

_____

_____

_____

_____

_____

_____

_____

Day 61

YOUR JOURNEY STARTS
. . . WHERE?

Have you ever thought about all the different ways you can get to where you want to go? Well, in life, we often discover that where we start often determines where we're going.

Proverb of the Day

> For the waywardness of the simple will kill them, and the complacency of fools will destroy them; but whoever listens to me will live in safety and be at ease, without fear of harm.
>
> *—Proverbs 1:32-33 (NIVUK)*

The invitation in this verse isn't wisdom or foolishness—it's wisdom or death. God makes it very clear when he references the Garden in verse 31 ("they will eat the fruit of their ways and be filled with the fruit of their schemes"), that a life without His direction only ends in eternal death. God is gracious to give us His Word and His ways, even in the form of man through the life of Jesus Christ, so let's not neglect it! God is calling out through His Word as our starting point. He says that if we listen, peace and comfort await us! So, let's choose to *start right* so we can end right!

JOURNAL

Day 62

ECHOES OF THE UNFILTERED MIND

Have you ever wondered if you could trust what someone said to you? People share things with us all day, but how do we know if they're trustworthy?

Proverb of the Day

Wisdom will save you from evil people, from those whose words are twisted.

—Proverbs 2:12 (NLT)

We live in a world filled with information we just blindly accept. We watch the news, read an article, and listen to messages, yet never question the source. Well, Jesus warns us what we take in is what comes out. So, if we're consuming what others have said, then others will say what they hear us say. We need wisdom to filter everything. If it doesn't align with His Word, no matter how "right" it may sound, we should back out.

> *Jesus warns us what we take
> in is what comes out.*

We need to allow God's wisdom to cleanse our ears and proceed with what Philippians 4:8 tells us to do: set our thoughts on whatever is noble, right, pure, lovely, admirable, excellent, and praiseworthy. This is how we avoid living with twisted thoughts!

JOURNAL

_____

_____

_____

_____

_____

_____

_____

_____

_____

_____

_____

Day 63

THE CURRENCY OF HONOR

Do you ever wonder whether your actions honored someone? We're often left feeling uncertain about how to measure honor.

Proverb of the Day

Honor the LORD with your possessions, and with the first-fruits of all your increase.

—Proverbs 3:9 (NKJV)

This verse removes the mystery of what it means to honor God—to release what most of us hold onto so tightly . . . our money.

> *God doesn't need our money;*
> *He desires our hearts.*

Statistics show that the last thing people who say they follow Jesus do is honor God with their finances. However, this shows God that we haven't truly given Him our hearts because of our trust issues. We struggle to trust that releasing what we see as ours belongs to the One who owns it all. The truth is, God doesn't need our money; He desires our hearts. We like to verbalize that we trust God, but trust isn't trust until it's been tested and acted upon according to the standards in which the measure has been set. When it comes to honoring God, the measure is our money. So, let's *remove the mystery* and show honor to the One who holds it all!

JOURNAL

Day 64

IT'S NEVER TOO LATE

Have you ever gone down a road and realized it was the wrong way? If so, you probably got a little gut check telling you this wasn't right. However, too often, we continue down that road, hoping it will get us headed back in the right direction.

Proverb of the Day

> Don't set foot on the path of the wicked or walk in the way of evildoers. Avoid it, don't travel on it; turn from it and go on your way.
>
> —Proverbs 4:14-15 (NIVUK)

It's like taking a wrong turn—we know we've gone down a path that doesn't lead to God because the Holy Spirit has told us. God loves us enough to always direct us back to Him!

> *No matter how far down the road we've traveled, God's road is still there.*

Unfortunately, despite this "gut check" from God, we tend to stick to our decisions because we're already here, so we might as well see how it turns out. However, that's a lie from the enemy who tries to keep us from what God has offered. Here's the truth: no matter how far down the road we've traveled, God's road is still there; all we need to do is stop and pay attention. He will get us back on the right course!

JOURNAL

_____

_____

_____

_____

_____

_____

_____

_____

_____

_____

_____

Day 65

DON'T LOCK THAT DOOR!

Have you ever thought to yourself: *I think I would enjoy being locked up in prison?* Probably not! There's no chance we would voluntarily step into that bare, cold, hard, uncomfortable room and lock ourselves inside that steel bar door.

Proverb of the Day

An evil man is held captive by his own sins; they are ropes that catch and hold him.

—Proverbs 5:22 (NLT)

Every day, people choose to step into a spiritual prison cell called sin. None of us would voluntarily walk into a physical prison cell, but in reality, the physical cell carries a lesser sentence than a spiritual one.

> *We need to remember that Jesus set us free.*

Most of us do all we can to stay out of the physical cell; the question is, do we make the same effort to stay out of the spiritual one? We need to remember that Jesus set us free. Let's make every effort to avoid stepping back into a cell we've already been set free from!

JOURNAL

_____

_____

_____

_____

_____

_____

_____

_____

_____

_____

_____

_____

_____

Day 66

YOU BECOME WHAT
YOU OBSERVE

H ave you ever considered that *observation is one of the greatest forms of education?* When you observe, you learn and gain knowledge that enables you to perform a task better than you could with only written information. I'm sure you've experienced this in your own life, and that is because you replicate what you see.

Proverb of the Day

Go to the ant, you sluggard; consider its ways and be wise!
—*Proverbs 6:6*

This verse invites us to observe things that will help us live life to the fullest. Even an ant can teach us something about life if we give it our attention.

> *We take on the nature of whatever gets our attention.*

So, the question is, if observation is one of the greatest forms of education, *what are you observing?* It would benefit us all to understand that we take on the nature of whatever gets our attention. Jesus tells us that *"the eye is the lamp of the body. If your eyes are good, your whole body will be full of light"* (Matthew 6:22, BSB). Every day, be sure to *observe healthy things with* your eyes; your life as a light for Jesus Christ depends on it!

JOURNAL

Day 67

THE LURE THAT LEADS TO RUIN

Have you ever thought, *that* will never happen to me! Often our famous last words, right? Why is it that so many of us view life through this lens?

Proverb of the Day

> For she has been the ruin of many; many men have been her victims.
>
> —Proverbs 7:26 (NLT)

Proverb 7 is about a father instructing his son to gain and keep wisdom so that he will stay away from their town's seductive woman. You and I may not deal with a seductive woman down the street, but we do deal with the lure of sin—even within the walls of our own home!

> *Sin has been the ruin of many, but it doesn't have ruin you!*

Sin comes in many forms and constantly calls our name. We think, there is no way it will happen to me, but consider this: have you ever found yourself behaving selfishly? If so, then "she's" lured you in because sin, no matter its form, is selfish at its core. Remember, sin has been the ruin of many, but it doesn't have to ruin you! We can *listen to wisdom* and avoid its lure!

JOURNAL

_____

_____

_____

_____

_____

_____

_____

_____

_____

_____

_____

_____

Day 68

STRAIGHT TO THE SOURCE

Have you ever needed information or answers to something? You knew that you could only get it from the one who owned it.

Proverb of the Day

Counsel and sound judgment are mine; I have insight; I have power.

—*Proverb 8:14*

Throughout our day, we often search for advice, good information, and insight about what we're walking through, and as this verse expresses, God owns these things. No one can offer better advice for life than the One who created it.

> *The need we receive from the Source comes with authority.*

We should turn to God before turning elsewhere in our search for wisdom today. If we do, we will also receive the other thing God owns

according to the verse: power! Power is the force behind authority—
the need we receive from the Source comes with authority. Why
would we shortchange ourselves by seeking what we need from
something or someone that doesn't give us the power to live it out?
Let's choose to *go to the source!*

JOURNAL

_____

_____

_____

_____

_____

_____

_____

_____

_____

_____

_____

_____

_____

Day 69

TUNE OUT HER VOICE

Have you ever noticed the world is full of noise, from music to animals, from machines to conversations . . . and so on? Often, where we are plays a role in how much noise we hear.

Proverb of the Day

> She [Folly] sits at the door of her house, on a seat at the highest point of the city, calling out to those who pass by, who go straight on their way.
> —Proverbs 9:14-15 (author addition)

We may not always be able to change our location, but we can tune our ears to what we need to hear—that choice is ours to make!

> ## *No matter where we are, God's wisdom is always there!*

We must be careful not to surround ourselves with too many voices; we need to be cautious in what we open our ears to because folly is always calling! Just as Folly—who is undisciplined and without knowledge—calls out to us, so does wisdom. No matter where we are, God's wisdom is always there! So, when we're not hearing what we should hear, chances are we need to check our surroundings and *tune accordingly.*

JOURNAL

_____

_____

_____

_____

_____

_____

_____

_____

_____

_____

_____

_____

_____

Day 70

THE PAYMENT THAT WILL NEVER BE DECLINED

Have you ever tried to purchase something with a form of payment you knew wasn't accepted? That's unreasonable, so chances are you haven't. It would make no sense to even try!

Proverb of the Day

Ill-gotten have no lasting value, but righteousness delivers from death.

—Proverbs 10:2

What we obtain can only be bought with what's accepted; nothing else will suffice. We can attempt to buy something with other resources, but at the end of the day, if it's not paid for the only way it can be paid for, you won't get what you intended to get.

Jesus is the only payment for everlasting life.

Every day, we have the opportunity to utilize the currency God gave us to pay for eternal life, and that's Jesus Christ. Why would we try to spend anything else to obtain this? Jesus is the only payment for everlasting life, so we need to stop trying to purchase it with things that don't work—ill-gotten and unaccepted things! Choose today to receive God's form of payment and obtain what only it can provide!

JOURNAL

_____

_____

_____

_____

_____

_____

_____

_____

_____

_____

_____

_____

_____

Day 71

DON'T LEAVE THEM GUESSING

Have you ever attended a live production? If so, you know the ending can make or break the whole experience. You'll either feel elated because the ending was just right or highly frustrated because it left you hanging.

Proverb of the Day

When the wicked die, that's it—the story's over, end of hope.
—Proverbs 11:7 (MSG)

When someone passes, we find ourselves either elated or frustrated depending on what we know or don't know. Sometimes, their story ends with sadness because, as our verse of the day tells us, a sad ending is just that—a sad ending.

> *Let's live that kind of life so that no one we leave behind has to guess our ending.*

The end of our lives doesn't have to be the end of our story. Jesus has given us all the choice to have a story that carries on in hope. Let's live that kind of life so that no one we leave behind has to guess our ending. Let's *live in such a way that our story of hope continues and our ending is clear*—leaving others elated!

JOURNAL

_____

_____

_____

_____

_____

_____

_____

_____

_____

_____

_____

_____

Day 72

THE PATH TO WISDOM IS PAVED WITH CORRECTION

Have you ever been told something that could change your life, and you had to decide whether to listen? The decision you make tells others a lot about the kind of person you are.

Proverb of the Day

Whoever loves discipline loves knowledge, but he who hates correction is stupid.

—Proverbs 12:1

In light of this verse, let's consider how we respond when someone corrects us. Do we get defensive and start an argument, or do we listen and apply the correction?

> *Throughout God's Word, those who accepted His discipline changed the world for His glory.*

The truth is, we should all consider how we react. This verse says that our unwillingness to receive correction reveals a lot about our intellect. Throughout God's Word, those who accepted His discipline changed the world for His glory. So, isn't it possible that avoiding "stupidity" and making a difference is based on our willingness to receive correction? Seems that way! Every day, let's choose to *gain wisdom and get better* for His glory!

JOURNAL

_____

_____

_____

_____

_____

_____

_____

_____

_____

_____

_____

_____

Day 73

SERVING UP WISE WORDS

Have you ever noticed that your attitude determines your experience at a restaurant? Consider how the words you use determine the meal you receive. You'll enjoy your favorite meal when you speak to your server with wise and kind words, but disruptive and rude words will lead to a bowl of slop. If you had known this, I bet you would have guarded what came out of your mouth so that you could enjoy what went in!

Proverb of the Day

Wise words will win you a good meal, but treacherous people have an appetite for violence.
—Proverbs 13:2 (NLT)

Interestingly, the effects of good words last about as long as a meal, but the bad words we use cause enough pain to have an ongoing effect. This is why it's so important that we watch what we say and continue to say!

✝

> *One wrong statement could disqualify us from being heard.*

One wrong statement could disqualify us from being heard, and more words of wisdom must follow one word of wisdom. Why is this? Because we have an enemy who is always trying to steal our voice. So, let's choose to *speak words of wisdom*, and watch how much you will enjoy the fruit they produce!

JOURNAL

_____

_____

_____

_____

_____

_____

_____

_____

_____

_____

Day 74

CONSIDER THE CONSEQUENCES

Have you ever had to do something because you made a bad decision that left you with no choice? Could it be because you should have done something before but didn't, and now your only option carries consequences?

Proverb of the Day

Evildoers will bow down in the presence of the good, and the wicked at the gates of the righteous.
                                        —*Proverbs 14:19*

"Evil" and "wicked" describe those who are, at their core, selfish; they choose themselves first every time. This kind of life has consequences, and these consequences are unavoidable.

Let's choose, in humility, to bow before our King now to remove the element of consequence.

The Word tells us that at the name of Jesus (the only One who is good), every knee will bow (Philippians 2:10). The Word also tells us that at the gate (into eternal righteousness), there will be weeping and gnashing of teeth (Matthew 13:42). Both will be unavoidable consequences for those who allowed selfishness to reign as king in their life. Let's choose, in humility, to bow before our King now to remove the element of consequence.

JOURNAL

Day 75

AGREEMENT IS AN ANTAGONIST

Have you ever asked someone for their advice but disliked what you received? Did it keep you from asking that person for advice the next time? Unfortunately, we tend to do that. We like to seek advice from those who agree with us. For most people, wisdom doesn't drive our search for advisers; agreement does.

Proverb of the Day

Plans fail for lack of counsel, but with many advisers, they succeed.

—Proverbs 15:22

What if, instead of rejecting those who disagree with us, we included them in the process and brought them alongside us to help us?

> *We need to realize that the wisdom we reject today may get us to where we're supposed to be tomorrow.*

The Bible tells us that true godly wisdom seeks to build up, not tear down. This means someone who loves God and cares for us will offer advice to help us live the life God has called us to live. We need to realize that the wisdom we reject today may get us to where we're supposed to be tomorrow. So, let's not let momentary emotions keep us from long-term success! Let's *seek godly counsel* and see our ideas and future flourish!

JOURNAL

_____

_____

_____

_____

_____

_____

_____

_____

_____

_____

_____

Day 76

FROM PRACTICE TO PURPOSE

Have you ever paused to think about how God has never relinquished the role of Creator of all things? Know this: the one who creates is the one who knows the purpose of that creation! We need to look no further than God Himself to know who we are and what we were made for!

Proverb of the Day

The LORD has made everything for His purpose!
—Proverbs 16:4 (BSB)

Every day, we get the opportunity to live this out! Jesus said the message of His life and purpose, was to lead God's creation to repentance (Matthew 4:17) so that eternal life could become our reality. That's His purpose. . . . what's yours? Why did God create you?

> *Our purpose in action is discovered in the practice of our efforts.*

First, we need to know this: it's to bring Him glory. You may not be sure what your purpose in action looks like, but you can be sure He wants to show you; remember, He created you for this! However, we need to know that our purpose in action is discovered in the practice of our efforts. So, we should ask ourselves: What efforts will we practice today to give God glory? We can rarely identify our position without practice, so let's go practice!

JOURNAL

_____

_____

_____

_____

_____

_____

_____

_____

_____

_____

_____

Day 77

TESTED TO BE TRUSTED

Have you ever taken a test? Of course, you have! Silly question! Like it or not, we all take tests, in some form or another, to assess our understanding so that we know where we go from there.

Proverb of the Day

Fire tests the purity of silver and gold, but the LORD tests the heart.

—Proverbs 17:3 (NLT)

Yes, you read that right: God tests us! But why? Because it's in these tests that He'll see where we go next. These tests reveal the impurities of our hearts, and from there, God can begin the process of helping us to remove them.

> *We should never look at testing as a problem but as an opportunity to promote our purpose.*

Going through tests to determine the condition of our hearts is crucial because our impure hearts can corrupt God's intended purpose. We should never look at testing as a problem but as an opportunity to promote our purpose. Let's learn to be okay with God testing our motives because the purer we are, the more valuable to His purpose we become!

JOURNAL

_____

_____

_____

_____

_____

_____

_____

_____

_____

_____

_____

_____

_____

Day 78

YOU WON'T FIND LOVE BEHIND WALLS

Have you ever bit into something bitter and said, "Oh wow, I love this!" Probably not! Bitter and love usually don't hang out together. However, for some reason, some live as if these words belong together when they claim love but display bitterness.

Proverb of the Day

An offended brother is more unyielding than a fortified city, and disputes are like the bars of a castle.
—Proverbs 18:19

When we allow bitterness to become our right, we shut out what God offers to make us right! (You should read that again.) Every time we protect the battleground of our bitterness, we add more bars to our lonely kingdom, keeping others out and rejecting love.

> *Those walls aren't keeping you safe; they're keeping you separated!*

Whether you're just now building walls or have already established a castle of bitterness, only you can tear down those walls to live in the love Christ has offered you. Becoming vulnerable again can be scary, but those walls aren't keeping you safe; they're keeping you separated! It's time to remove the walls of bitterness and let God become your place of protection. There's life outside the walls!

JOURNAL

_____

_____

_____

_____

_____

_____

_____

_____

_____

_____

_____

_____

_____

Day 79

CURB YOUR ENTHUSIASM

Have you ever known someone whose enthusiasm leads them to make lots of mistakes? They mean well, but their enthusiasm tends to be their demise. It's like a young child who's excited to do something on their own, like pour milk, but they end up pouring it all over the counter and floor. If we're not careful, we can easily do this in life.

Proverb of the Day

Enthusiasm without knowledge is no good; haste makes mistakes.

—Proverbs 19:2 (NLT)

Enthusiasm isn't bad; however, it must be controlled and guided.

> *Biblical knowledge coupled with righteous action equates to godly wisdom.*

Enthusiasm comes in different forms—confidence, eagerness, and zeal—however, action without knowledge results in chaos. But the answer isn't to lose your enthusiasm; the answer is to *gain the knowledge* needed to guide it. We also need enthusiasm for knowledge to become action; if not, our knowledge will waste away. Biblical knowledge coupled with righteous action equates to godly wisdom. So yes, let's be excited—but excited to see our actions work for God's glory!

JOURNAL

Day 80

THROW THE RIGHT ROCK

Have you ever seen a ripple effect? Maybe you've stood on the edge of a pond and tossed a rock into the water. The rock transfers energy to the water molecules, causing them to move and create successive waves beyond the point of contact. This process carries on until the energy dissipates and the effect fades away.

Proverb of the Day

The godly walk with integrity; blessed are their children who follow them.

—Proverbs 20:7 (NLT)

Our actions create energy that causes ripple effects beyond the starting point. Chances are, you've experienced this from those who came before you. Good or bad, you've probably felt the actions of your parents, grandparents, or someone else.

> *Our actions establish blessings and curses, but they can also end them.*

Actions aren't momentary; what we do today affects our future and the future of those to follow us. So, we should ask ourselves: Would I desire my actions or would I despise them? Our actions establish blessings and curses, but they can also end them. Let's make integrity-based actions that generate blessings for those who will follow. If you think you've already caused curses, there's still time; change your actions to change the future!

JOURNAL

_____

_____

_____

_____

_____

_____

_____

_____

_____

_____

_____

Day 81

LEND YOUR EAR TO GET HIS

Have you ever wanted God's attention—like, you *really* wanted Him to hear you? Well, there's an answer for how to make this happen. God clarifies throughout His Word how we can ensure our words are heard.

Proverb of the Day

If a man shuts his ears to the cry of the poor, he too will cry out and not be answered.
> —*Proverbs 21:13 (author paraphrase)*

When we only care to hear what we want to hear, then God won't hear what we want Him to hear.

> *If we want our voices to reach the ears of the Lord, then we must lend ours to those in need.*

The ears of a selfish man only speak words from a selfish heart; however, God isn't interested in our selfishness! He's interested in *us*, just not our selfishness. If we want our voices to reach the ears of the Lord, then we must lend ours to those in need. This could be our spouse, children, co-workers, or anyone who needs attention; that's what the word "poor" represents—someone in need. *When we lend our ear; we reach God's!* Today, let's open our ears and hear those around us—the attention we need depends on it!

JOURNAL

Day 82

THE ULTIMATE ROI

Have you ever thought about your life's ROI—return on investment? If I invest two things and get back three, that's a 50 percent return on my investment. Rarely can you find that kind of return anywhere, but we can find it in the Kingdom of God!

Proverb of the Day

Humility and the fear of the LORD; its wages are riches, honor, and life.

—Proverbs 22:4

Do you see the investment you need to make to get the return you're hoping for? The investment is humility and reverence to God, and He will return wealth, honor, and life!

> *Choose to give God humility and reverence, not for the return, but because He's worthy of it.*

If we humble ourselves, He enhances our abilities; if we revere Him, He lifts us up; and as an increase, He gives us life! There is no greater place to invest our life than in the life of Jesus Christ! Every day, choose to give God humility and reverence, not for the return, but because He's worthy of it. You do this with a pure heart and clean hands; He will give you a return that will never end—life eternal! Now, let's *make the investment!*

JOURNAL

_____

_____

_____

_____

_____

_____

_____

_____

_____

_____

_____

_____

Day 83

WORDS THAT START A PARTY

Have you ever said something so meaningful to someone that they couldn't help but celebrate, such as good news to a parent or promises for a child? Many words can bring great joy to other people. Did you know that God celebrates your words . . . when they are good?

Proverb of the Day

Everything in me will celebrate when you speak what is right.

—*Proverbs 23:16 (NLT)*

His Word, the Truth of Jesus Christ, is a perfect example of what is right.

> *God loves it when His kids testify to what He has done.*

When we speak about what Jesus has done in our lives, He celebrates because we're taking what we've received and sharing it with someone else to strengthen them. God loves it when His kids testify to what He has done and talk about their Savior. Today, let's speak what's right, it may cause someone to choose Christ; then there will be a party in heaven and the angels celebrate! So, let's cause a party!

JOURNAL

_____

_____

_____

_____

_____

_____

_____

_____

_____

_____

_____

_____

Day 84

THE TAKER'S TRAP

Have you ever heard the phrase, *there's no honor among thieves?* This saying means that even a thief can't trust a thief, and in life, there are only two types of people: those who give and those who take.

Proverb of the Day

> Do not envy the wicked, do not desire their company;
> for their hearts plot violence, and their lips talk about
> making trouble.
>
> —Proverbs 24:1-2

Every day, we're faced with the decision of the kind of people we will be: givers or takers.

> *Jesus and His faithful followers*
> *will never plot against you.*

It seems like an easy decision; however, it's also easy to get caught up in wanting what those who live according to the world's standards want, but that's a trap. The trouble the trap creates will hurt us more than we know! The only way to avoid the snare is to not play the game of wicked men but live according to the ways of Christ! Jesus and His faithful followers will never plot against you because *there's honor among the righteous!*

JOURNAL

_____

_____

_____

_____

_____

_____

_____

_____

_____

_____

_____

_____

_____

Day 85

USEFUL OR USELESS?

Have you ever had to decide what to allow into your life, knowing your decision will determine how useful you can be? Every day, we will either be effective or ineffective depending on what we allow into our lives.

Proverb of the Day

Take away the impurities from the silver, and there comes out a vessel for the smith.

—Proverbs 25:4 (NASB)

We should all take the time to examine the impurities we've allowed into our lives because they may be the very thing keeping us from being useful in the hands of God. Just as with silver or gold, we become more valuable when the impurities are removed! The Bible tells us that this is up to us; we are to choose purification, purify our hearts, wash our hands, and take captive our thoughts—the choice is up to us!

> *We become more valuable when
> the impurities are removed!*

So, the question is: are *we* willing to *remove our impurities*? If not, then we're telling God we like our impurities more than His purposes. Choose today to *purify for the purpose!*

JOURNAL

_____

_____

_____

_____

_____

_____

_____

_____

_____

_____

_____

Day 86

DON'T FUEL THE FIRE

Have you ever heard the phrase, you're adding fuel to the fire? Have you ever been guilty of it? And I'm not talking about a literal fire but an emotional one. Chances are, you have done this, especially if you've ever been in an argument.

Proverb of the Day

> Without wood a fire goes out; without a gossip a quarrel dies down.
>
> —Proverbs 26:20

That's a pretty obvious observation: a fire can't burn without fuel. It will burn until all the fuel is gone, but once it's gone, so is the fire.

> *Fires compromise the infrastructure of what it burns.*

When we find ourselves in a quarrelsome situation, the quarrel lasts only as long as we fuel it. This means that what you say can control how long a quarrel lasts. If you fuel it with more negative or inflammatory gossip, expect the fire to rage. But know this: fires cause damage, and that damage leads to a lack of trust because fires compromise the infrastructure of what it burns. This is why it is important to put out fires as soon as possible! If you face a quarrelsome situation today, *starve the fire and minimize the damage!*

JOURNAL

Day 87

MOTIVES THAT DISARM THE ACCUSER

Have you ever found yourself proud of a child you raised who lived their lives according to how you taught them? When this happens, you stand a little taller and are more confident to face whatever may come.

Proverb of the Day

Be wise, my son, and bring joy to my heart; then I can answer anyone who treats me with contempt.
—Proverbs 27:11

As children of God, walking in His wisdom and living according to His ways brings joy to His heart!

His heart grieves when He sees that what we want from Him fuels our motives.

Satan's role was the accuser of God's people, telling God that we only worshiped Him because of what He could do for us. As a dad, it hurts when I discover that my kids did something I asked of them only to get something from me. In the same way, His heart grieves when He sees that what we want from Him fuels our motives. Today, let's choose to be the son or daughter who promotes love for our Father in the face of the accuser! *Live in such a way that brings joy to our Dad's heart!*

JOURNAL

_____

_____

_____

_____

_____

_____

_____

_____

_____

_____

_____

Day 88

NEUTRAL ISN'T NEUTRAL

Have you ever done nothing only to discover that doing nothing is doing something? In life, there is no middle ground; we either do or we don't.

Proverb of the Day

> Those who forsake the law praise the wicked, but those who keep the law resist them.
> —Proverbs 28:4 (BSB)

At times, we may find ourselves avoiding a decision to maintain neutrality, but our lack of decision implies we support something.

> *How we live our life exemplifies a life for or not for Christ; if we don't live it, we haven't kept it!*

When it comes to living a life for Christ, there is no such thing as a neutral position. Essentially, we could phrase the verse this way:

those who forsake Jesus praise the wicked, but those who keep Jesus resist them. Either way, every action is a supporting choice. In the Old Testament, people exemplified the law by the life they lived; if you didn't live it, you weren't keeping it. But the same goes for us even today—how we live our life exemplifies a life for or not for Christ; if we don't live it, we haven't kept it! There is no middle ground. Let's go out today and *say the right things—not just with words, but through how we live!*

JOURNAL

_____

_____

_____

_____

_____

_____

_____

_____

_____

_____

_____

Day 89

WHO DO YOU THINK YOU ARE?

Have you ever thought about who you are to God? Who you think you are matters a lot because our perspective determines our approach to life. Do you see yourself as a servant or as a son/daughter?

Proverb of the Day

Servants cannot be corrected by mere words; though they understand, they will not respond.

—Proverbs 29:19

There's a real struggle between having the mind of a servant and that of a son or daughter. A servant struggles with instructions because they lack the relationship that drives the request.

> *The relationship determines where you'll lay your head down when the work is finished!*

Throughout life, our relationship with our leaders often determines how we handle the work in front of us. The servant and the son usually have the same responsibilities, but the relationship determines where you'll lay your head down when the work is finished! So, if it takes more than God's Word to get your attention, maybe it's because of how you view your relationship. It's time to *be a son and not just a servant!*

JOURNAL

_____

_____

_____

_____

_____

_____

_____

_____

_____

_____

_____

Day 90

CHECK YOUR REFLECTION

How do you view yourself regarding sin? Do you see yourself as someone without imperfections or as someone who needs to be purified?

Proverb of the Day

> *Those who are pure in their own eyes and yet are not cleansed of their filth.*
>
> —*Proverbs 30:12*

If we desire, we can approach life pretending that our sin is nothing more than a problem to be corrected instead of an implication of separation that must be removed.

> *How we view ourselves will determine the posture we take before God.*

When we think our sin isn't an issue, then we'll also think we can stand before God in pride instead of being on our face before Him in humility! The truth is that how we view ourselves will determine the posture we take before God. There's a great phrase that says, A man on his face can't fall from that place. Every day, to avoid a prideful mind, we must evaluate how pure we think we are and respond accordingly! Chances are, *our response should be face down!*

JOURNAL

_____

_____

_____

_____

_____

_____

_____

_____

_____

_____

_____

_____

_____

Day 91

THE GOOD BRIDE

Have you ever paused to consider your responsibility as the bride of Christ? Don't worry; most of us don't. However, in our role as the future bride of Christ, there is something we should focus on that would bring Him honor.

Proverb of the Day

She brings him good, not harm, all the days of her life.
—*Proverbs 31:12*

We should all ask ourselves: Are my actions the kind of actions that bring Him good? Now, we can't answer this according to our perspective; we need to answer this according to His righteous observation. However, for this to take place, we must realize that our actions can't be responsive; they must be predetermined.

> *Our actions can't be responsive; they must be predetermined.*

As the bride of Christ, there will be plenty of times when we're not in the mood to bring Him good, but we don't fulfill our responsibilities according to our emotions; we fulfill our responsibilities according to His design. We must know that if we choose Him as our Savior, we also choose ourselves as His bride. It's time we fulfill the role and *bring Him good!*

JOURNAL

_____

_____

_____

_____

_____

_____

_____

_____

_____

_____

_____

_____

_____

www.ingramcontent.com/pod-product-compliance
Lightning Source LLC
Chambersburg PA
CBHW070536090426
42735CB00013B/3001